See how they grow

Pets

DK

Goldfish

My mother has lots of tiny eggs.
Inside each one, a little goldfish is growing.
One of them is me!

Goldfish eggs

2

I am a newly hatched fish.
I carry around a yolk sac
that I feed on as I swim.

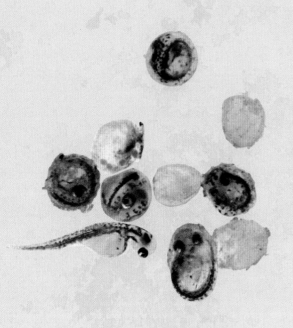

Hatched

Three days

My yolk sac has gone and I can eat on my own now. I'm growing fins. My colour is changing too.

Six days

Four months

4

I am fully grown! I swim around all day long. My golden scales shimmer and shine in the water.

Adult goldfish

Rabbit

I'm a sleepy newborn rabbit.
I live in this cosy nest.
My mother made it
from straw and fur.

Newborn

My skin is pink, but soon soft, white fur begins to grow. I crawl along with my tummy close to the ground.

One week

Two weeks

Three weeks

My fur is thick now. When it gets messy, I lick myself clean.

Four weeks

Five weeks

I'm growing big and strong.
My ears are growing too.
I'm still not as big as my
mum, though.

Six weeks

Mother rabbit

Kitten

I have just been born.
I am still wet and cannot
see or hear. My mother
feeds me and licks me dry.

I open my eyes and I can see!
I'm starting to hear and smell things too.
I learn to crawl, sniffing as I go.

One day

Four days

Two weeks

I am growing bigger every day.
I can now prance, prowl, and pounce.
I love to play.

Four weeks

Six weeks

I've learned to clean myself too,
just like grown-up cats. I lick my paws
and use them to brush my fur.

Eight weeks

Ten weeks

Puppy

I am a newborn puppy.
I smell my mother's milk
and crawl to her to drink it.

14

I snuggle and sleep all day, dreaming of milk.
I open my eyes, but soon fall asleep again.

One week

Two weeks

I am growing quickly.
I can walk very well now.

Four weeks

Six weeks

Off I go to explore. Everything I find is new and interesting.

Eight weeks

Pony

I am a foal,
a newborn pony. This
is my mother. She feeds
me her warm milk.

My legs are wobbly at first,
but I grow stronger every day.
Neigh! I can even call out loud.

Newborn

Two weeks

I play and run around in the field.
When I feel hungry, I eat grass
or crunchy apples.

Five weeks

Eight weeks

My coat has changed. It's a deeper, chestnut brown. I'm getting big, but I'm still growing.

Four months

Five months

How did they grow?

Goldfish

Rabbit

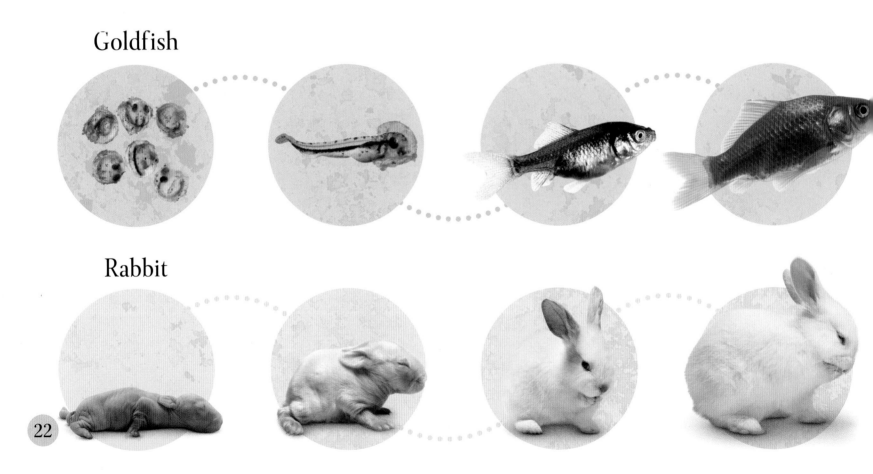

Kitten

Puppy

Pony

Editor Sally Beets
Senior Editor Roohi Sehgal
Assistant Editor Gunjan Mewati
Project Art Editor Kanika Kalra Grover
Designer Charlotte Jennings
Jacket Designers Rachael Hare, Dheeraj Arora
Jacket Co-ordinator Issy Walsh
DTP Designers Sachin Gupta, Vijay Kandwal
Picture Researcher Vagisha Pushp
Production Editor Abi Maxwell
Production Controller Francesca Sturiale
Managing Editors Jonathan Melmoth, Monica Saigal
Managing Art Editors Diane Peyton Jones,
Romi Chakraborty
Delhi Creative Heads Glenda Fernandes,
Malavika Talukder
Publishing Manager Francesca Young
Creative Director Helen Senior
Publishing Director Sarah Larter

First published in Great Britain in 2021 by
Dorling Kindersley Limited
DK, One Embassy Gardens, 8 Viaduct Gardens,
London, SW11 7BW

The authorised representative in the EEA is
Dorling Kindersley Verlag GmbH. Arnulfstr. 124,
80636 Munich, Germany

A CIP catalogue record for this book
is available from the British Library.
ISBN: 978-0-2414-7009-1

Printed and bound in China

For the curious
www.dk.com

ACKNOWLEDGEMENTS

The publisher would like to thank the following for their kind permission
to reproduce their photographs:
(Key: a-above; b-below/bottom; c-centre; f-far; l-left; r-right; t-top)

1 **Dorling Kindersley**: Barrie Watts (bl). 2 **Dreamstime.com**: Verastuchelova (bl). 2–21 **Dreamstime.com**:
Galina Drokina (Background). 3 **Dreamstime.com**: Verastuchelova (br). 4 **Dreamstime.com**:
Verastuchelova (bl). 5 **Dreamstime.com**: Verastuchelova (br). 6 **Dorling Kindersley**: Barrie Watts (bl, crb).
7 **Dorling Kindersley**: Barrie Watts (clb, cb, crb). 8 **Dorling Kindersley**: Barrie Watts (br, clb).
9 **Dorling Kindersley**: Barrie Watts. 22 **Dorling Kindersley**: Barrie Watts / (bl, bc/One week, bc, br).
22–23 **Dreamstime.com**: Galina Drokina (x20). 24 **Dorling Kindersley**: Barrie Watts / (crb)

Endpaper images: *Front:* **Dorling Kindersley**: Barrie Watts bl; *Back:* **Dorling Kindersley**: Barrie Watts bl

Cover images: *Front:* **Dorling Kindersley**: Barrie Watts cla; **Dreamstime.com**: Galina Drokina;
Back: **Dorling Kindersley**: Barrie Watts fcla, cla, ca, ca/ (3 weeks), tr; **Dreamstime.com**:
Galina Drokina; *Spine:* **Dorling Kindersley**: Barrie Watts

All other images © Dorling Kindersley
For further information see: www.dkimages.com

MIX
Paper from
responsible sources
FSC™ C018179

This book was made with Forest
Stewardship Council™ certified paper –
one small step in DK's commitment to a
sustainable future. For more information
go to www.dk.com/our-green-pledge